FLAMINGOS
by Liza Jacobs

BLACKBIRCH®
PRESS

San Diego • Detroit • New York • San Francisco • Cleveland • New Haven, Conn. • Waterville, Maine • London • Munich

LIBRARY OF CONGRESS CATALOGING-IN-PUBLICATION DATA

Jacobs, Liza.
    Flamingos / by Liza Jacobs.
        v. cm. -- (Wild wild world)
    Includes bibliographical references (p. 24).
    Contents: About Flamingoes -- Cleaning and Preening -- Flamingo Food --
Mating -- Growing Up.
     ISBN 1-4103-0035-8 (hardback : alk. paper)
    1. Flamingos--Juvenile literature. [1. Flamingos.] I. Title. II.
Series.

    QL696.C56J33 2003
    598.3'5--dc21   2002154165

Printed in Taiwan
10 9 8 7 6 5 4 3 2 1

Table of Contents

About Flamingos

Flamingos live in warm areas such as the Caribbean. They also live in parts of Europe, Africa, and India.

They are found in marshes and swamps that lie next to saltwater.

There are a few different kinds of flamingos. They vary in color, but all a shade of pink.

Flamingos range from 4 to 5 feet high and weigh up to 9 pounds. Th have very long legs, webbed feet, and downward curved beaks.

Flamingos like to live in very large groups, called flocks. Although th are social birds, flamingos will honk and snap at each other if one crowds too close.

4

Cleaning and Preening

These beautiful birds are good swimmers and graceful fliers.

To keep their feathers in tip-top shape they carefully clean, or preen, them. First, a flamingo flaps and ruffles its feathers in the water. Then stretches and twists its long neck to reach different parts of its body. uses its beak to comb and pick through dirt and lay its feathers flat.

A flamingo's foot can be used to scratch hard to reach head feathers.

The black feathers seen on outstretched wings are a flamingo's flight feathers. It is very important to keep these feathers working well. Aft all that preening, a flamingo is ready to fly.

Strong Fliers

Flamingos are large birds. In order to get their bodies in the air, they need to get a running start.

A flamingo begins by walking, and then picks up the pace. It unfolds its wings, running and flapping. Flamingos almost look as if they are running on top of the water just before they take to the air.

They are strong birds and can fly long distances without taking a rest. When they fly, they keep their legs stretched out straight behind them.

Flamingos can fly up to 35 miles per hour!

Flamingo Food

Flamingos eat a variety of small water plants, insects, and shrimp-like shellfish.

Many of the foods flamingos eat have the same substance in them that make carrots orange. By eating these foods, flamingo feathers become pink. If a flamingo is not fed these foods, its feathers will become white again. This sometimes happens in zoos.

No matter what their shade of pink, all flamingos have black-tipped beaks and black flight feathers.

A flamingo eats in an unusual way—with its head upside down! It takes in a mouthful of food and water. Then it uses its tongue to push the water out through tiny filters along its bill, or beak. This lets a flamingo separate food from mud and salt water. Flamingos feed in both shallow and deeper waters.

Napping and Resting

Flamingos take naps at any time of day.

They often sleep standing on one leg, with their head tucked under a wing. Flamingos do this for two reasons. From this standing position, it is faster to fly away from danger. Removing most of its body from the water also helps the bird stay warm.

Flamingos will also curl up and sleep on dry ground.

13

Mating

To communicate with each other, flamingos make loud honking sounds. They sound a lot like geese.

During mating season, flamingos make more noise than usual. A male attracts a female by honking. If she approves, she honks back.

A pair of flamingos often does a courtship dance before mating.

There is a lot of flapping, feather ruffling, and honking!

Nesting

These social birds like to stick together—even when they are nes

When a female is ready to lay her egg, she builds a tall mound of
mud. To do this, she piles up mud, pounding and packing it with
feet and beak to make it solid. The male flamingo helps scoop ou
shallow top so the egg doesn't fall off the sides. These nests can l
up to 16 inches high. Being higher helps keep water from floodin
the nest.

A flamingo usually lays 1 egg in her nest.

The male and female take turns sitting on the nest for about a month.

Baby Chicks

Flamingo babies are called chicks.

Like other birds, chicks have a special egg tooth on their beak. This is used to help a chick break out of its shell.

Flamingo parents stay close while the chick hatches. Chicks are born with long legs like their parents. But their bills are straight, instead of curved. Chicks are covered with warm, soft, gray down.

Both male and female flamingos produce a special milk to feed their chicks. This rich, reddish milk comes from glands in the throat. A chick drinks the milk from its parent's bill.

Growing Up

Within a month, a chick's bill starts to curve downward.

It grows more feathers on its wings and body.

Within 2 months, chicks can find food by themselves.

Like their parents, chicks like to gather in groups.

Parents are always close by to make sure the chicks stay safe.

Ready to Fly

By the time it is 3 months old, a chick has grown enough flight feathers to be able to fly.

It rests on one leg and sits with its legs bent backward just like its parents.

Chicks will not develop their pink feathers until they are 3 or 4 years old. At that time, they are ready to mate and start families of their own.

For More Information

Hewett, Joan. *A Flamingo Chick Grows Up.*
    Minneapolis, MN: Carolrhoda, 2001.

McMillan, Bruce. *Wild Flamingos.* Boston,
    MA: Houghton Mifflin, 1997.

Switzer, Merebeth. *Flamingos.* Danbury, CT:
    Grolier, 1990.

Glossary

bill beak

flock a group of flamingos

preen to clean feathers